PRESENTED BY  INSIGHTFUL BOOKS

ROCKET SCIENCE FOR YOUR LITTLE ONE

MINUTELY ILLUSTRATED COLORFUL JOURNEY OF A BABY, RILEY! WITH PROPER PARENT NOTE!

In the end, an unique surprise is waiting for you!

FOR BUSINESS ENQUIRIES EMAIL AT: "UNIQVISE@GMAIL.COM"

Rockets are big machines that fly into space. They are tall, thin, and have engines that push them up very fast. Rockets can carry astronauts, satellites, or supplies.

Hi! This is Riley. Do you know how rockets work?

And this is my memento batch that I got from tour at NASA!

Riley: Rockets are like big, powerful cars that can drive into space. They have engines that give them lots of energy to lift off the ground and go up, up, up!

PARENT NOTE -
Rockets: Big machines that fly into space using powerful engines.

When a rocket blasts off, it's called lift-off. The rocket engines burn a lot of fuel to make the rocket go up, away from Earth. This creates a lot of smoke and fire at the bottom of the rocket.

Have you ever seen a rocket lift off on TV or in a video?

Riley: Lift-off is when a rocket starts its journey into space.

It's very exciting and loud because the engines are working hard!

PARENT NOTE -

Lift-off: When a rocket starts flying into space.

Rockets need special fuel to make them fly. The fuel is stored in big tanks and burns to create hot gas. This hot gas pushes the rocket up into the sky.

ROCKET FUEL TANK

What do you think rocket fuel looks like?

BACKGROUND OF ABOVE QUESTION TELLS THE COLOR!

Riley: Just like cars need gas to go, rockets need special fuel. When the fuel burns, it makes a lot of hot gas that helps the rocket lift off.

PARENT NOTE -

Fuel: Special stuff that burns to make rockets fly. As more oxygen in body helps you to run faster, same way Rocket too!

Gravity is a force that pulls everything towards Earth. Rockets need to work very hard to overcome gravity and fly into space. This is why they need so much power.

Ground-grabber AKA Gravity

STRONG

Riley: Gravity is what keeps us on the ground. Rockets need a lot of power to push against gravity and go into space. Can you jump high?

While both gravity and the magnetic field are crucial for life on Earth, they operate independently of each other.

Imagine how strong a rocket has to be to fight gravity!

PARENT NOTE -

Gravity: The force that pulls things towards Earth, formulated by Albert Einstein.

Thrust is the force that pushes rockets up into the sky. The rocket engines create thrust by burning fuel, which makes the hot gas push down and the rocket go up.

Riley: Thrust is like a big push that helps rockets fly. The engines make thrust when they burn fuel, which pushes the rocket into the sky.

GAS IS PUSHED OUT & BALOON IS PUSHED UP

Like a balloon zooming around when you let go!

THRUST PUSHES ROCKET UP

HOT GAS PUSHES DOWN

PARENT NOTE -

Thrust: The force that pushes rockets up into space.

Rockets have different parts called stages.
Each stage has its own engines and fuel.
When a stage uses all its fuel,
it falls away, and the next stage takes
over to help the rocket go higher.

Actually, Riley is inside this Rocket!

How many stages do you think a rocket has?

Riley: Rockets are built in parts called stages. Each stage burns its fuel and then falls away to make the rocket lighter.

HI! I AM ONE OF THE SUSPENDED STAGE OF ROCKET FLYING ABOVE!

PARENT NOTE -

Stages: Different parts of a rocket that help it go higher.

The payload is what the rocket carries into space. It can be satellites, astronauts, or supplies. The payload sits at the very top of the rocket.

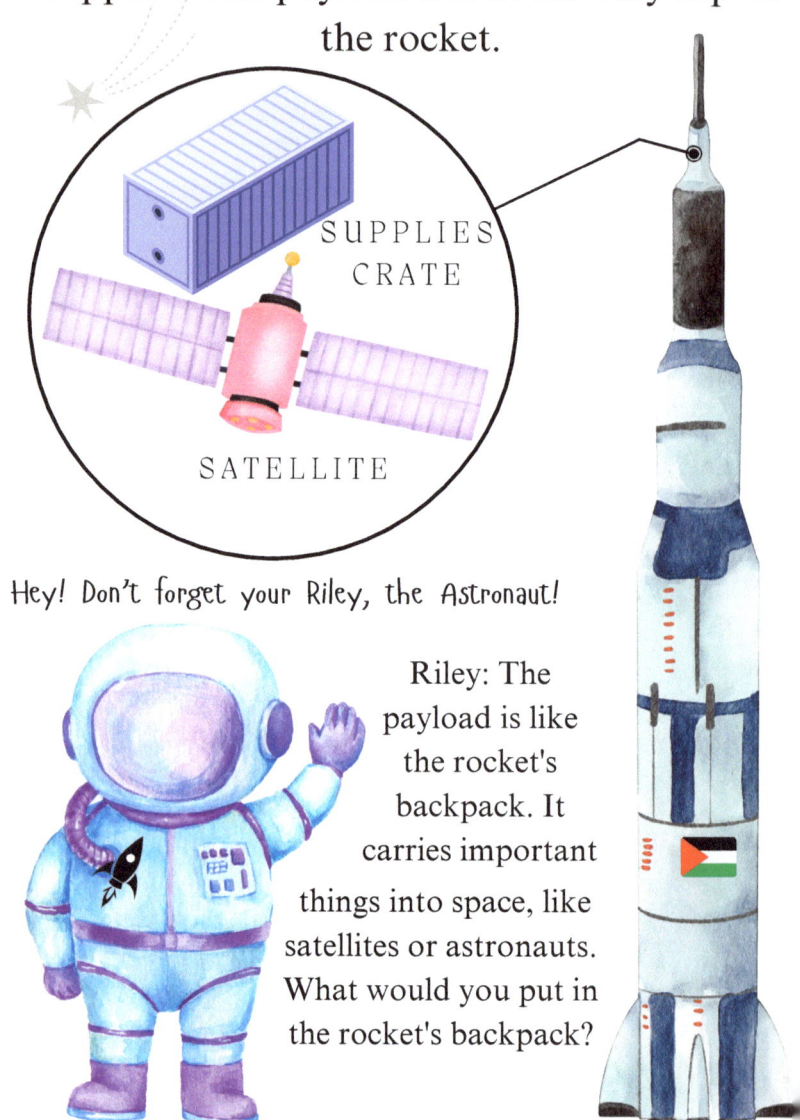

SUPPLIES CRATE

SATELLITE

Hey! Don't forget your Riley, the Astronaut!

Riley: The payload is like the rocket's backpack. It carries important things into space, like satellites or astronauts. What would you put in the rocket's backpack?

PARENT NOTE -
Payload: What the rocket carries into space.

Rockets have a guidance system to help them know where to go. It uses computers and sensors to make sure the rocket follows the right path to space.

Riley: The guidance system is like a rocket's brain, telling it where to go and how to get there.

But this!

Buddy not this

"Have you ever used a treasure map to find your way around like an explorer?"

Like us even Rockets got their Brain.

PARENT NOTE -

Guidance System: A system that helps rockets know where to go. like a rocket's special map to reach space!

The rocket nozzle directs the hot gas out of the engine to create thrust. It is shaped like a cone and helps control the direction of the rocket.

Riley: The nozzle is like a hose for the rocket's engine. It directs the hot gas to push the rocket up. Have you seen a hose spray water?

NOZZLE

The nozzle works in a similar way!

SPLASH!

PARENT NOTE -

Rocket Nozzle: Part of the rocket that directs hot gas to create thrust.

Trajectory is the path a rocket follows to reach space. It's planned carefully to make sure the rocket gets where it needs to go. This helps the rocket avoid obstacles and reach its destination.

FOLLOW THE PATH

Riley: Trajectory is like the rocket's travel plan, showing the path it will follow to reach space.

Do you like to plan your trips and know where you're going?

Trajectory: The path a rocket follows to reach space.

PARENT NOTE -

Rockets start their journey from a special platform called a launch pad. The launch pad holds the rocket steady and has equipment to fuel and check the rocket before lift-off.

Riley: The launch pad is like a big, sturdy stage where rockets start their journey. It's strong enough to hold the rocket until it's ready to fly.

Have you ever imagined putting an Earth flag on a distant planet?

PARENT NOTE -

Launch Pad: A special platform where rockets start their journey.

Fairings are the protective covers that shield the payload during launch. They keep it safe from air pressure and heat. Once in space, the fairings fall away.

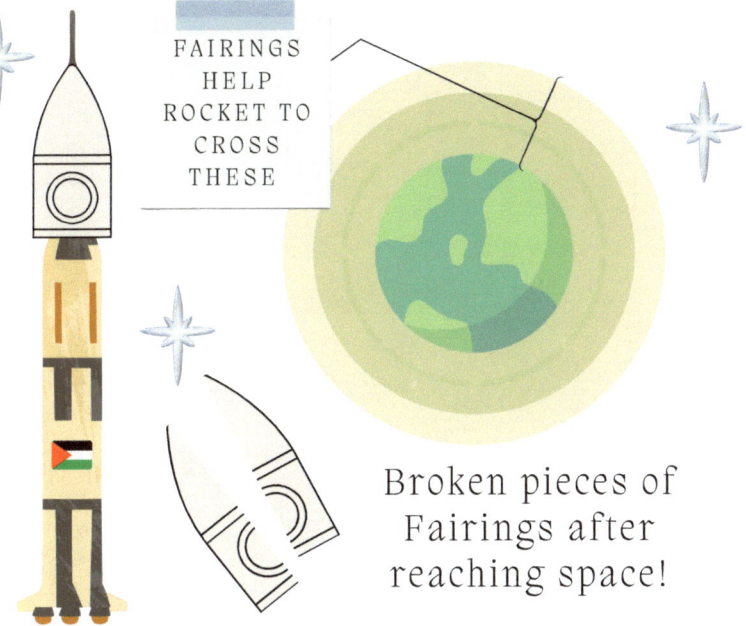

FAIRINGS HELP ROCKET TO CROSS THESE

Broken pieces of Fairings after reaching space!

Remember that same way like you take off your jacket when it's warm outside, a rocket removes its fairing in space to stay cool and light.

Fairings: Covers that protect the rocket's ayload during launch.

PARENT NOTE

LIKE THAT OF AN ATTACKING ARMY!

Riley: Boosters are like extra muscles that help the rocket lift off. They give extra power and fall away when they're done.

You see, more or less like muscles of bodybuilder. We don't have those muscles but we can still lift loads of normal weight but can we lift 800 pounds of weight, probably not!!

The spacecraft is the part of the rocket that goes into space and carries the payload. It can carry astronauts, satellites, or experiments. The spacecraft separates from the rocket once it's in space.

In the context of space missions, "experiments" refer to scientific tests and research conducted in the unique environment of space.

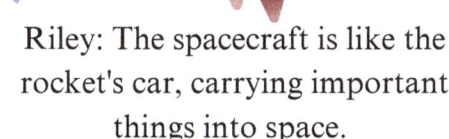

Riley: The spacecraft is like the rocket's car, carrying important things into space.

Spacecraft: The part of the rocket that goes into space and carries the payload.

PARENT NOTE -

Rocket engines burn fuel to create thrust, pushing the rocket into space. They are very powerful and can produce a lot of energy. The engines are carefully designed to be strong and efficient.

THIS BEAST IS OUR ROCKET'S ENGINE

AFTER ENGINE IS OUR NOZZLE!

They are powerful enough to lift the rocket all the way to space!

Riley: Rocket engines are like the rocket's heart, burning fuel to make it fly. Can you imagine how strong a rocket engine is?

PARENT NOTE - Rocket Engines: Engines that burn fuel to create thrust and push the rocket into space.

Mission control is the team of people who help guide and monitor the rocket's journey from Earth. They watch the rocket's progress and make sure everything goes as planned.

ROCKET'S LANDING POINT

Do you like working in a team to accomplish something important?

Riley: Mission control is like a big team of helpers making sure the rocket's journey goes smoothly. They watch and guide the rocket.

PARENT NOTE -

Mission Control: The team of people who help guide and monitor the rocket's journey.

Before a rocket lifts off, there is a countdown. The numbers count down from ten to zero, and then the rocket launches! The countdown makes sure everything is ready.

COUNTDOWN

Riley: The countdown is like waiting for a race to start. When it gets to zero, the rocket takes off.

Have you ever counted down before starting something exciting?

PARENT NOTE -

Countdown: The numbers that count down to zero before a rocket launches.

Some rockets can land back on Earth. They use engines or parachutes to come down safely. This helps them to be reused for future missions.

Riley: Rocket landing is like a gentle touchdown after a big jump. Rockets use engines or parachutes to land safely.

Ever wondered how satellites return to Earth with a smooth landing?

PARENT NOTE -

Rocket Landing: Rockets coming back to Earth safely using engines or parachutes.

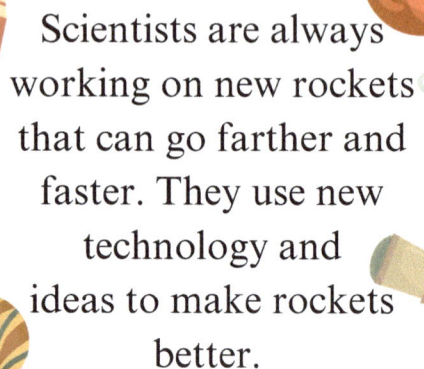

Scientists are always working on new rockets that can go farther and faster. They use new technology and ideas to make rockets better.

Riley: The future of rockets is like dreaming about new adventures. Scientists are always making rockets better. What do you think rockets will look like in the future?

PARENT NOTE - Future Rockets: New rockets that scientists are working on to go farther and faster.

from the bottom of my heart, Thank you!

UNIQVISE

is my initiative to spread authentic and simplified informations in an unique and to the point talks. I am an university student and looking forward to change myself and elevate the condition of current chaotic world with the help of the Creator, the one! Catch me at instagram account: "UNIQVISE".

LITTLE NOTE

FOR BUSINESS ENQUIRIES EMAIL AT:
"UNIQVISE@GMAIL.COM"

CUT OUT THIS CERTIFICATE AND DECOR YOUR CHAMP ROOM!

MINI DIPLOMA IN ROCKET SCIENCE

This certifies that

_____

has begun exploring the exciting world of Rocket Science! For your stellar advancements in early exploration!

"CURIOSITY IGNITES ROCKETS OF POSSIBILITY IN THE MINDS THAT DARE TO DREAM."

Date of Issuance:
_____

WRITE ABOVE BABY'S NAME & DAY YOU REACHED HERE!

CUT OUT THIS CERTIFICATE AND DECOR YOUR CHAMP ROOM!

www.ingramcontent.com/pod-product-compliance
Lightning Source LLC
Chambersburg PA
CBHW041512010526
44118CB00006B/231